2/17/11.

To Terry.

Please keep shining your
light. THIS WORLD NEEDS
you.

Know you're loved and honored

Dr K Gordon

MIND &
MANIFESTATION

A Compilation of Articles
November 2007 - January 2010

DR. KENNETH D. GORDON

Mind & Manifestation - A Compilation of Articles
Copyright © 2010 by Dr. Kenneth D. Gordon

www.cslkelowna.com

Editor-in-Chief: Dr. Deborah J. Gordon
Publisher: Stephanie A. Blue

ISBN: 145055654X

Acknowledgments

I would like to acknowledge so many people who have been influential in my life but, due to space, I will limit it to those few who have been so influential in this book. So, in no particular order, here goes: Dr. Cynthia Cavalcanti, the Editor of Creative Thought magazine, who never fails to make me sound clever. Corinne Crockett, who is so thorough her additional editing allows me to appear educated. Stephanie Blue my publishing agent, who inspired me to put the book together and patiently guided and directed the entire project. To my beautiful wife, Dr. Deborah Gordon, who has loved me and supported me for over three decades and who I can truly say always leads me from behind. In addition, the Centre for Spiritual Living - Kelowna, at which every member and friend is my support. The Board of Directors of ICSL, specifically Dr. Candice Becket and Dr. Jim Lockard, who are my sister and brother in life. My daughter Kelsey Corbett and son Mackenzie Gordon, who have always been my teachers. And finally, last but not least, my grandson Cooper and his soon-to-be-born brother, "Brother Baby," who are my constant reminder as to why I do what I do: Awaken Humanity!

Please know that you are loved, honoured and recognized. Blessings, Dr. Kenn Gordon

Declaration of Principles

What We Believe
By Dr. Ernest Holmes

We believe in God, the Living Spirit Almighty; one indestructible, absolute, and self-existent Cause. This One manifests Itself in and through all creation, but is not absorbed by Its creation. The manifest universe is the body of God; it is the logical and necessary outcome of the infinite self-knowingness of God.

We believe in the incarnation of the Spirit in Us, and that all people are incarnations of the One Spirit.

We believe in the eternality, the immortality, and the continuity of the individual soul, forever and ever expanding.

We believe that heaven is within us, and that we experience it to the degree that we become conscious of it.

We believe the ultimate goal of life to be a complete freedom from all discord of every nature, and that this goal is sure to be attained by all.

We believe in the unity of all life, and that the highest God and the innermost God is one God. We believe that God is personal to all who feel this indwelling presence.

We believe in the direct revelation of truth through our intuitive and spiritual nature, and that any person may become a revealer of truth who lives in close contact with the indwelling God.

We believe that the Universal Spirit, which is God, operates through a Universal Mind, which is the Law of God; and that we are surrounded by this Creative Mind which receives the direct impress of our thought and acts upon it.

We believe in the healing of the sick through the power of this Mind.

We believe in the control of conditions through the power of this Mind.

We believe in the eternal Goodness, the eternal Loving-kindness, and the eternal Givingness of Life to all.

We believe in our own soul, our own spirit, and our own destiny; for we understand that the life of all is God.

Contents

Foreword

You will find that the articles contained herein are written
in the first person. This writing and speaking style
was chosen so that the reader may identify directly
in mind with the concepts described.
You may accept these words as your own, if you choose.

Notes

Note pages have been provided throughout this book for
reflections, scribbles, musings and contemplations.
Sometimes our notes are divinely inspired and
these pages are there to capture intuitions.
A history of evolving consciousness is thereby recorded.

Enjoy!

Introduction

Dr. Kenneth D. Gordon bases his teachings on the New Thought philosophy founded by Dr. Ernest Holmes in his ground-breaking work "The Science of Mind: A Philosophy, A Faith, A Way of Life" ©1938. This philosophy is now taught in centres around the world, known as the Centers for Spiritual Living™.

These articles present a fresh concept of spirituality as a life philosophy. Dr. Kenn is currently the President of International Centers for Spiritual Living™, as well as the spiritual director for the Centre for Spiritual Living in Kelowna, British Columbia, Canada. The vision of Dr. Kenn and his wife, Dr. Deborah Gordon, has created a community that is now the spiritual home to many like-minded people taking part in workshops, classes and Sunday services.

This compilation is a collection of short articles published during Dr. Kenn's term as President, from November 2007 to January 2010.

Notes

Grateful and Happy
November 2007

When I was an active ski patroller and the temperature would drop to more than 30 degrees below zero (before the wind chill), I often found myself assigned the task of going to the most inhospitable parts of the mountain to check the few skiers braving the weather for signs of frostbite. Inevitably, conversation between the skiers, other patrollers, and myself would turn to how cold it was. Every word spoken focused on the temperature, or lack of it. Within minutes, I would find myself shivering, stomping, whining, and freezing with the best of them.

Knowing full well I was exacerbating the situation, I developed a little ritual I would use at times like these. When the opportunity arose, I practiced the following routine: I would remove my toque, take off my balaclava, open my jacket to my waist, and stop and feel the cold. I would sit in this position of undress for two or three minutes and just allow the cold to penetrate every pore of my exposed body. I would close my eyes and breathe, feeling the dryness and biting wind run through me. I would endure the cold and wind and counsel my body not to shiver or react.

After a few minutes, I would fasten my jacket and replace my gear. The warmth would return and flow through my body, and with it came an awareness of where I was and a remembrance of the gratitude for being there. I would reawaken from the small and inconsequential discomfort and consciously allow myself to return to reality, fully and completely present in nature, healthy, strong and vital, in the midst of the most awesome beauty life can display. The cold would recede back into its true proportion, and my perspective would turn to the wonder and gratitude of life.

My teacher, Dr. Tom Costa, used to say, "You cannot be grateful and unhappy at the same time." What I have found is that I cannot be grateful and poor at the same time, I cannot be grateful and sick at the same time, I cannot be grateful and unfulfilled at the same time, and I cannot be grateful and unloved at the same time. Everywhere I look, I find there is more to be grateful for than not. There is more energy, more abundance, more opportunity, and more love than not.

With Thanksgiving time and the approach of Christmas, we have the opportunity to be reminded of the massive gift life is. No matter the situation, there is more to be grateful for than not. It is up to us to take this opportunity and open ourselves to the reality of our lives so we can adjust our attitudes to see and experience the riches, joys, and gifts that lie at our feet.

The practice is simple: Take the time to open up, remove your protection, and let the condition appear for what it really is. Then, hold it up and let it dwindle in comparison to the abundance that waits for your awareness. Take the good that surrounds you and put it on like a warm winter jacket. Do not let this opportunity pass you by.
Be grateful.

Notes

Notes

The Meaning of the Season
December 2007

December is the month with the fewest hours of daylight in the year, a time of darkness, dormancy, and sleep. To the ancients, it must have been a time of angst, questioning the rebirth of the forms of life that were necessary to sustain and maintain their very existence. The absence of both sun and vitality of growth must have been terrifying to a culture that had a superstitious understanding of the laws of life.

Many religious beliefs were derived from such circumstances. These beliefs provided people with the hope of rebirth and continuation of everything required to support what they understood. From this place, the celebration of the winter solstice and, by extension, Christmas and other December festivals were born, celebrations that marked a renewal of growth and a regeneration of the vitality and energy of existence.

Science of Mind is a spiritual philosophy that brings to light the laws of life. Religion provides an avenue for hope, science proves the principles of living, and spirituality brings those principles into focus in the life of the individual through intuition. The three join together to define a Divine recipe, which, when followed, results in a complete and whole understanding of our existence. Our founder, Dr. Ernest Holmes, wrote, "Revelation must keep faith with reason, and religion with law–while intuition is ever spreading its wings for greater flights–and science must justify faith in the invisible."[1]

We are past the superstitious consciousness and corresponding fear of winter being the end of life. Evolution and reason provide us with proof of an ongoing goodness that comprises all the chronological phases of life. We understand that our beautiful planet will continue to revolve around our magnificent sun, and that January will provide more light than December just as December provides less than November. We have replaced superstition with a revelation of reason. So why continue the celebration?

At this time every year, we celebrate a new revelation, a new consciousness, and a new idea–one that moves us away from angst and fear as it proves itself in our lives. This is the time we instill hope in humankind for greater understanding. In this day and age, in this season, we continue to celebrate a knowing that everything required to sustain our lives returns as we celebrate the coming of the light.

Now is the time we need to advance a new hope–a hope in Peace on Earth and goodwill to humankind. This is the meaning of the season. Portray it as you will. Describe it in any way it will be heard. Celebrate it in any manner that will awaken the intuitive knowing of its reality. Awaken the revelation in all who can hear. It is our responsibility as Religious Scientists to instill hope in humankind. Hope for peace, hope for understanding, hope for love, and hope for all.

Notes

1 - Holmes, E. (1938). *The Science of Mind. A philosophy, a faith, a way of life.* Penguin Putnam Inc: NY (p. 25)

Notes

Happy New Year
January 2008

Recently, I read a wonderful story about a two-day hike just outside Banff, in the Canadian Rockies. Apparently, there is a famous hiking trail there known for both its rigor and its beauty. Quite a distance up this steep and mountainous climb is a chalet. Generally, it is reached at around noon on the first day of the two-day ascent, and it is here that climbers stop for lunch, take their boots off, and take a well-deserved rest.

The owner of the chalet says it happens the same way almost every time. After stopping, eating, and resting for an hour, the guide gathers the climbing party and gets them ready to resume the trek. He says there are always a few who ask about accommodations, and when they learn the chalet is a full service hotel with rooms, fireplaces, and food, they announce to their climbing companions that they are going to stop there and wait for their fellow climbers to complete the ascent and return the next day.

It is interesting, he says, to watch the ones who choose to stay behind poke fun at the ones who continue on into the freezing weather and brutal climb. As the climbers head out for the remainder of the excursion, the ones who stay behind seem to naturally drift over to the windows and gaze at the hillside. The laughter and good-natured jibes slowly turn to silence, and the ones remaining begin to look longingly at their companions on the slopes as they become small specks in the distance. As the afternoon and evening wear on, they return time and again to the windows, spotting the climbers as they make ready for night and picking out the campfires as darkness falls.

The next morning, there is usually none of the laughter of the previous afternoon. There is no joy or excitement. They have breakfast then sit by the window until noon, when the returning climbers burst through the doors. The ones returning are cold, tired, and hungry, but they thrill with the sense of accomplishment.

As they leave the chalet together, the difference in the two groups is palpable. One group is vitalized and empowered and can hardly wait to get to the bottom to share their experience with their family and friends. They have a story to tell. The ones who spent the night in the chalet are quiet and meekly walk behind.

What is new for you this year? What do you want? What is your intention, and are you going to follow through with it? Are you going to brave the rigors and potential discomfort of achievement, or are you going to pass up the opportunity to participate in this magnificent life? Activity, accomplishment, and action create energy. Everything we desire depends on this energy, and our job is to direct it with intention. Why not give of yourself this year? Why not step up and make the climb and become a full participant in life? Make this the year you reach the top.

Notes

Notes

A New Idea
February 2008

I once attended a class conducted by Dr. Raymond Charles Barker. In it, he candidly shared that when he found himself faced with a seemingly insurmountable issue, he would go into his den, sit, and say, "Barker, you need a new idea!" I like that alot and use it all the time. Every challenge I have ever faced is contained within an old idea, some residual belief I constructed, adopted, and implemented into my life. Most beliefs served a purpose at some point but the effect remains static until I expand the idea behind it. Evolution is the first law of growth, and ideas need to expand just as form needs to change.

I love the story of the man who goes to a tailor and has a new suit made. During the fitting, he notices one of the sleeves is two inches too long, so he asks the tailor to take it in. "No, we don't need to," says the tailor, "just bend your elbow and it pulls up your sleeve." "Okay," says the man, "but look, when I do that, the collar goes four inches up my head." "No problem," says the tailor, "just raise your head up and tilt your neck back, there, now it is perfect." "Yeah," replies the man. "But now this shoulder is lower than this one." "Easy!" says the tailor, "just bend at the waist and lean over, and it all evens out."

The man leaves the store wearing the suit with his elbow crooked and his head sticking out, up, and back while

leaning to one side. The only way he can walk is with a
slight limp while twisted to the side, which gives him kind
of a push-and-drag gait. As he walks down the street, he
passes two men standing at a corner. The first says, "Look
at that poor crippled guy, my heart really goes out to him."
The second man says, "Yeah, but look at that suit–it fits him
perfectly."

So it is in our lives. We often find ourselves trying to fit an
old idea into a new situation, and far too often, society
tells us we simply need to adapt to the form. One of the
great values Science of Mind brings to the world is a
recognition that things do not have to be the way they are.
As Religious Scientists, we are called upon to be catalysts
to awaken individuals to a new idea. Our churches are
called to awaken our communities to a new idea, and as an
organization, we are called to awaken the world to a new
idea. Every challenge has a solution; every solution begins
in the consciousness of the one or ones who are aware there
is another way.

I have no doubt that the majority of this planet yearns for
peace, harmony, abundance, and equality. Maybe we do not
have it because the majority of the world does not believe it
is possible. Maybe they do not think it is possible because
they believe they need to compromise and fit an old idea
into a new form. We know better. What the world needs is a
new idea.

Notes

Notes

Step into the Mystery
March 2008

Science of Mind begins with the premise that it is done unto us as we believe. In the past, when I believed it was done unto me according to the vagaries of society, my family of birth, my educational status, or how much money I had, etc., I found experiencing joy and abundance entailed struggle and toil. Without an understanding that my experience depended on growing my belief, I spent inordinate amounts of time attempting to change the effect of my life without ever experiencing anything different. The result was struggle, pain, and effort, after years of which I began to feel hopeless and unfulfilled. It was only when I discovered the Science of Mind teaching that I began to grow and discover a life of direction and fulfillment. The longer I practice this, the more I understand it is all consciousness.

Consciousness–with a small "c"–means the sum total of my belief, both conscious and unconscious. Last month in my article, I referred to Dr. Raymond Charles Barker's method of dealing with "supposed" insurmountable issues. It was his practice to start with an awakening affirmation, namely, "Barker, you need a new idea!" When faced with a desire for anything other than what I currently perceive, I am required to establish a new idea about who I am and what I want so I can move into receptivity for a new experience. Once this is established, everything else shows up in order for me to embrace this new manifestation.

You cannot get any simpler than that. The issue ceases to be, "How do I make the form fit me?" and moves to, "How do I make myself grow to fit the form?" Though simple, I do not always find it easy.

William James stated, "A great many people think they are thinking, when they are merely rearranging their prejudices."[1] A prejudice is a preconceived opinion. Far too many times I have made the mistake of taking my preconceived opinions with me into my Spiritual Mind Treatment and inner contemplation. I have approached the "supposed" insurmountable issue from the same foundation of thought that supported its existence in the first place.

To change unproductive behavior, I am learning to surrender. My spiritual practice begins with the conscious suspension of any opinion, regardless of whether I believe it supports my desired experience or not. I am learning to willingly give up cynicism. I joyfully affirm that anything is possible in the Infinite Mind.

If you are currently experiencing an insurmountable issue, whether it is a present-moment crisis or an ongoing unsatisfactory effect, I recommend you consciously suspend all opinion you have around it. Accept that whatever you think you know about it is only a minute portion of what is really true. Step back from it and say to yourself, "I need a new idea around this!" Then, pay attention. A new idea is always more than an old idea rearranged; however, to arrive at it, we must consciously surrender what we think we know is true and step into the mystery.

Notes

1 - James, W. (n.d.). BrainyQuote.com. Retrieved June 23, 2010 from BrainyQuote.com website: http://www.brainyquote.com/quotes/quotes/w/williamjam109175.html

Notes

Evolving Self-awareness
April 2008

A life of honesty and introspection, while often challenging, is rewarding. It is not always easy to observe our own deepest and most hidden prejudices and judgments. The reward is a life of purpose, choice, self-direction, and freedom. The challenge is to maintain clarity in that purpose, to establish and implement said clarity through our choices, and to take full responsibility for every experience in our lives.

I find one of the impediments to doing this is the fact that I actually have prejudices and judgments stacked on top of my already-prejudiced judgments. Here is an example: The other day, I had a little bout of pettiness when I stopped to help a woman who had tipped her wheelchair over and was lying helpless and crying in the snow. After struggling to get her and her motorized chair back on the sidewalk, I discovered she could actually walk and was quite mobile. My sense of her seeming entitlement and infringement on my time enraged me. After my little fit of indignation, I recognized thoughts that ran through my head during the incident: anger, resentment, disgust, and a sense of being manipulated and taken advantage of.

This is not who I want to be. As I recognized these feelings, the next thought followed, and it had to do with self-reproach. Every feeling I was projecting toward the woman came back upon me, highlighting my own self-deception and self-criticism.

How could I–this supposed loving, caring person who presumably has entered into a commitment to spend myself in service to humanity–feel this way?

This is what I mean by judgment stacked on judgment, i.e., my judgment of someone else and my judgment of myself for judging. In the past, I may have justified my opinion of being manipulated and blamed the woman, or blamed myself by justifying my own lack of compassion. Both would be inaccurate and ineffective. Clearly, it was not about her, so it must have been about me–or is there a third option?

There is another thing to know: just as what I think about the woman is not true, what I think about myself is equally delusional. It is as erroneous to blame myself as it is to blame the woman.

Each of us is an expression of the Thing Itself evolving into self-awareness. We are not our thoughts. We are responsible for them, but we are not them. Inner spiritual work is not about aligning ourselves with a thought even when the thought is who we think we are. It is about aligning ourselves with Spirit.

While being responsible for our beliefs is a critical step in this process, we must always remember our beliefs are not who we are. To paraphrase Dr. Holmes, the only thing that ever needs to be healed is a sense of separation from God. When we blame or judge, we separate from our Source. The answer is to be aware of the denigrating opinion, remind ourselves of the greater Truth, and remember the awareness of our Divine Nature is curative.

Notes

Notes

Looking Up
May 2008

There were once two young boys who lived on the banks of the Chekamus River. Every year at spawning time, the river turned red with salmon swimming upstream. Just before the fish began to run, the availability of such abundance attracted thousands of bald eagles who perched on the tops of the trees bordering the river.

One year, marveling at the many beautiful birds, the two youngsters decided they would trap one and make it their pet. They built a cage from lodge poles and included a large trapdoor on the top. They then went to the riverbank with a large net and waited. When the fish began to run, they hid quietly in the woods until one of the eagles dove from its lofty perch to grab a big, fine salmon in its talons. Just as the bird touched the water, they cast their net and trapped it.

They took the eagle, squealing and struggling, to the cage and placed him through the trapdoor into his new home. The eagle was furious. He dropped down into the enclosure and hopped immediately to the side facing the boys. There, he clung ferociously to the poles and screamed in outrage. The youngsters were very pleased they had caught such a brave and powerful pet and they determined they would tame him. However, as the days went by, the eagle clung to the cage and continued to voice his anger and rage, striking out at every opportunity to harm them when they came near and taking neither water nor food. After a week, the boys grew fearful for the eagle's life and soon decided they must set him free.

That afternoon, fearful the eagle would harm them, one distracted the bird in its cage while the other climbed to the roof and opened the door. The two then retreated out of sight so the bird could escape. The eagle never moved. In his fury, he clung to the bar and continued raging. Days passed, and even though the cage was open and the eagle was free to escape, he never moved from his spot. He continued to cling to his position, raging and attacking, not taking any food or water until in time, he weakened and died.

There are times in our lives when we are like the eagle, living our lives in anger, rage, and fear. Often, I have found certain beliefs I hold–even though based on valid experiences–have imprisoned me. When I become willing to stop my story long enough to look up, I discover that I, in fact, was freed long ago.

The eagle in this story is so fixated on his captors that he does not realize he is free. What am I so fixated on that it blocks my ability to see another option? What do I hold so dearly to be true that I attach myself to the experience? What am I so invested in that I will not let it go?

Whatever it is, Science of Mind assures us it is not immune to Truth, and the Truth is always an open trapdoor to freedom. All the eagle needed to do was step away from the bars and look up. All we need to do is step back from the issues that restrict us and look up. In our teaching, we call this a spiritual practice. I do it daily because for every cage, there is always a door.

Notes

Notes

A Living Idea
June 2008

A living idea in the Mind of God has inherent within it everything required to grow and flourish. It does not require you, me, or anyone else to maintain it. It derives all its requirements from First Cause–Spirit. On more than one occasion in my life, I have struggled to maintain a form that disappeared as soon as I turned my back on it. This was a living idea in my mind and required everything in order to maintain it–not from Spirit but from me. While I am certainly part of Spirit, when I feed an idea that is not of the One, it drains and depletes me. Hospitals are filled with people keeping ideas alive that are not of the One. War is another example of a depleting idea, one that cannot sustain itself over a long period of time. Forced creative expression and unhappy work conditions drain and deplete the individuals subjected to them. A relationship bogged down in "have tos" and "must dos" that are against the nature of the participants are exhausting. Huge rewards come from the practice of moving in the flow with a living idea. The challenge is matching our wants, desires, opinions, and direction with the flow of Infinite Intelligence. So, I ask myself, 'How do I live my life in the flow?' The answer is to have faith, forgiveness, and surrender.

Faith is knowing everything is created with a purpose and that purpose contains within it everything required to sustain it–even me. Forgiveness means taking back my power and letting go of my story, no matter how real or right I think it is. I must erase my story from my vernacular, excise it from my belief system, and banish it from my concept of reality because it is limiting my potential.

Surrender is simply allowing my higher power to supersede my individual knowing. This means expecting an experience that charges me with energy and rejecting any concept that drains it. It is not about trying to save energy, but instead starting to spend myself with knowing that as I give, everything returns to me in abundance. It is also about sharing myself in unconditional service.

The best place to practice this formula is among like-minded individuals, and the best place to find them is at a Religious Science church or centre. Our churches and centres were created as living ideas in the Mind of God for the purpose of awakening individuals to their own spiritual magnificence. There, you can expect to be filled by realizing (real-izing) God in your life.

I have absolutely nothing more important to do than to be my authentic self. I would suggest this is true for you as well.

Notes

Notes

Embracing the New
July 2008

So much change, so many new ideas, and so much to do–the Universe is always tilted toward enhancement. An acorn becomes an oak tree, a child becomes an adult, rain becomes a river, a bulb becomes a flower, an idea becomes a thing, fear becomes enlightenment, and consciousness continues its ever-moving process of flowing toward Truth.

As Religious Scientists, we believe the essence of a thing does not exist in its form but in the thought that precedes it. Accepting the expansive nature of life, it seems obvious that what we think today must be enhanced and expanded in form tomorrow. It stands to reason that an idea I know as true in this minute is a shadow of potential in the next. The Universe conspires to evolve.

In 1994, at Whitefish, Montana, Religious Science International set an intention in the form of a vision. It was to "Awaken Humanity to its Spiritual Magnificence." At that time, we did not know how to do it beyond what we were already doing. No one would have predicted the process that followed. Fourteen years later, we witness our world in transformation. Science of Mind, as an integral part of what is known as the New Thought movement, has participated in the awakening of millions of people, and we find ourselves on the threshold of the next monumental step in our unfoldment.

This month at our annual conference at Asilomar, we will once again come together to reaffirm and share our vision with each other. There are so many topics and so many changes going on at this time that it is almost impossible to keep them in order or remember how they came to be. However, we do know each and every one of them is a direct manifestation of our vision. Integration with our brothers and sisters in the United Centers of Spiritual Living includes a branding process shared between the two organizations, a new conference schedule with avenues to serve the world, an empowered and developing web and IT presence, new ideas around sharing and teaching in developing countries, reaching receptive new markets, and a new curriculum being produced. All this stems from one intention set by a small group of individuals, that was then established, directed, and nourished.

The Universe enhances, and what we know to be true today is actually a limited reflection of what is true tomorrow. The only thing that could possibly slow down this process is ourselves. I can think of a thousand obstacles and another thousand made-up reasons why this cannot or should not continue to happen; I refuse to accept them. There is something greater at work here, something more powerful, more present, and clearer than what I know today. I am willing to trust the process and continue to allow it to unfold, for I have absolutely nothing better to do than to awaken both myself and others by extension.

My intention is to continue to trust Spirit and to know It always enhances. What is required of me is to do what is before me and get my limitations out of the way.

Notes

Notes

Communication and Inclusiveness
August 2008

It is the desire and mandate of our organization to grow and develop inclusiveness and communication while always acting from the principles we espouse. Having an inclusive organization, attitude, or intention essentially means we are conscious that there is space for everyone. Communication means everyone has a voice, everyone is heard, and truth, openness, and transparency are the normal practice. Being in principle indicates that we operate from an intention of love, unity, self-direction, and self-responsibility in every thought, word, and deed.

Being open and inclusive allows new ideas and new opinions to be formed; it opens doors to greater ideas than those previously held. Its inevitable effect is newness and growth, and if it is growth we want, then these virtues serve as tools to precipitate, develop, and facilitate that growth–personally and organizationally.

Staying in principle in the midst of communication and inclusivity is sometimes a different story altogether. It is not hard for me to imagine how much easier it would be to stay in principle if I were to live a solitary life, communicating only with myself. I am always astounded at how easy I am to get along with when there is only me to reflect and share with, and in turn, what a challenge it can be to live in love, unity, self-direction, and self-responsibility when I am interacting with others. Living only with my own opinion retards my growth, while living in community precipitates it. It is the interaction with others that provides the playing field for newness.

Werner Heisenberg, the quantum physicist who devised the Uncertainty Principle, said real advances are made at the intersection where two different lines of thought meet.[1] In other words, real growth comes from more than one disparate or divergent idea or opinion coming together to birth a third.

Living, working, loving, disagreeing, and even disliking create a medium for the development of newness and growth. When I am open to more than just my own opinion, I grow.

At the intersection of two thoughts, a third is automatically born. It is not that one is right and one is wrong; it is that when combined, they produce a third that is greater than either of the originals. It is evidence of the mind evolving.

You do not have to agree with me. It is enough to simply be receptive to hearing me. In that action lies the seed of self-knowing and growth. The Infinite lies in repose, awaiting our discovery, and is birthed in all our interactions.

Notes

1 - Heisenberg, W. (1927). English Translation. J.A Wheeler & H. Zurek. *Quantum theory and measurement.* Princeton University Press: New Jersey, 1985. (pp. 62-84)

Notes

Principle Formula
September 2008

The principle is simple: Thought + Feeling = Form. Knowing the truth of life's goodness, prosperity, enhancement, and love is to be in integrity with Spirit. Knowing what I think and how I feel about any situation and honoring that is to be in integrity with myself. We can never enter into unity with God until we first achieve unity with our own self. Denial and repression do not change the form; they simply reinforce the principle. My thought plus my feeling equals my form.

I teach this concept to my students using this illustration: if I think I am going to step outside my front door and get hit by a bus, I do not step out the front door. Often the response I hear is, "Yes–but that isn't the truth." They are partially right. It is not God's Truth. However, as long as it is my truth, it has the same effect.

A problem I used to have was thinking there was "right and wrong" belief. I believed I would appear "less than" if I honestly expressed what I knew I thought and felt versus what I thought I should think or feel. I would compromise my own truth, limited as it was, when I would pretend it was not so in order to appear more spiritual or more powerful than I actually believed I was. The result inevitably would leave me feeling like I had been hit by a bus. This occurred because the form always matched what I really thought, not what I thought I should think.

There is only one way to rise above a false belief and become what we are rather than what we think we should be. We do this by uncovering and changing our false ideals and aligning them with Truth. I use three tools to accomplish this: Spiritual Mind Treatment (affirmative prayer), self-contemplation, and meditation. I call these tools my spiritual practice.

The purpose of spiritual practice is to align our thinking and feeling with the attributes of Spirit for the purpose of bringing into form the consciousness of Truth. The purpose of Spiritual Mind Treatment or affirmative prayer is to direct our thoughts to what we want to recognize in form. The purpose of self-contemplation is to awaken to our own truth; the purpose of meditation is to awaken to God's Truth. The purpose, ultimately, is to replicate the Life of Spirit in our own lives.

Dr. Ernest Holmes said Spiritual Mind Treatment is clear thinking. Self-contemplation is a clear receptivity to the "what and why" of my thoughts and feelings, meditation is to converse and be open to ideas from the Absolute within. All these practices are undertaken with the same purpose–to become one with ourselves and one with God.[1]

My thought plus my feeling equals my form. The form of my life is a direct projection of this concept. As I step outside my front door, I encounter whatever I expect to encounter. Today, I expect the good.

Notes

1 - Holmes, E. (1938). *The Science of Mind. A philosophy, a faith, a way of life.* Penguin Putnam Inc: NY (p. 638)

Notes

A Personal Purpose
October 2008

A personal purpose for life is probably the most gratifying of all intentions. When fulfilled, it motivates and attracts everything else. When not fulfilled, it represses, depresses, and repels everything that brings joy to the individual.

I did not always know this. I used to think that what was missing in my life could be solved by having more stuff. Last month, I referred to my own personal spiritual practices: contemplation, meditation, and Spiritual Mind Treatment. The thing about these spiritual practices is that I did not start them with the intention to recognize or uncover a personal purpose for life; I began in order to get something. As I developed, I found the stuff I thought was the answer was not filling the void. No matter; I am still grateful for that mistaken belief because it moved me to practice, and practice awakened me to the real solution.

Many of us came to this teaching seeking a means to make our material lives richer and found instead that our inner lives were enriched. Many began with a belief that material things were missing and having more stuff would fill the emptiness we felt. And why not? We, in Western society, have been taught we can, and indeed should, have all the material good of life. Inherently, we know this is not true. If having things were the answer, we would be the happiest

people since time began. We live in the wealthiest society
that has ever existed, and still, there is a gnawing within us
that seems to be ceaseless. In the tenth century, the ruler of
Spain, Caliph Abd-er-Rahman III, said:

> Riches and honors, power and pleasure have waited
> on my call, nor does any earthly blessing appear to
> have been wanting to my felicity. In this situation,
> I have diligently numbered the days of pure and
> genuine happiness that have fallen to my lot. They
> have numbered 14.[1]

Two weeks is not much of a payoff for having everything,
but it does prove once again that looking outside ourselves
for the answer is not the answer. Disciplined practice of
self-knowing and Spirit-centered connection, no matter why
it is instigated, inevitably evolves into something greater.
An original pursuit of pleasure and stuff becomes a larger
view of connection and contribution to life. The desire
for personal preferences is never lost. What we discover is
these preferences direct us to the practice that slakes the
unquenchable thirst for purpose.

Spiritual practice uncovers our connection with all and
facilitates the evolution of our individual consciousness to
the recognition of the real value of life. When you see this in
your day-to-day experiences, your days are filled with pure
and genuine happiness.

No matter what path you take to discover your spiritual
good, if it is true, it leads you to yourself. Spiritual practice
is self-knowing.

Notes

1 - Peterson, E. H. & Niles, R. (2007). *The great pursuit: the message for those in search of God.* Nav Press: Colorado Springs, Co.

Notes

Interesting Times
November 2008

The adage, "May you live in interesting times," is said to be both a blessing and a curse. I suspect the choice is ours. We do live in interesting times.

Anyone who is even slightly awake today must be aware of the monumental changes that appear to be affecting our planet, culture, organizations, politics, and relationships at this time. Global warming, consumerism, corporate restructuring, political unrest, changing job markets and styles, and an evolving definition of family structure is apparent everywhere we turn. As the world evolves, nature flows in its own way, society makes demands that reflect change, time and space expand and contract, and the flexible excel while the static struggle.

It is the purpose of spiritual community to provide sanctuary from the latter. I do not mean sanctuary that impedes the process. I am talking about the kind that supports individuals in understanding and evolving to a place in awareness and truth that permits them to go with the innate flow of life and to direct it for the benefit of all.

I once read that the next great leap forward in the evolution of our race will be moving from the consciousness of competitiveness to one of creativity. At the time, I was not sure how that change would or could take place. I see it now. We have been inculcated into a world where competitiveness has been absorbed and has dominated every aspect of our civilization. Competitiveness has been around for so long that we take for granted it is a natural way, if not the only way, to live. We compete for resources, market share, love and affection, power, approval, and to be right. Our nations compete, as do our communities and families. We compete as individuals. Even our limited concepts of spirituality compete. There is so much energy expended in competition it is a wonder we have come as far as we have.

We have all the technology, resources, intelligence, and love required to move into a world capable of providing everyone and everything with a joyful, light-filled, fulfilling, productive, caring, and supportive existence that works in harmony with our planet, others, and life. The only thing missing is the reason to do so. The Universe is giving us a not-so-gentle nudge in the direction of Truth. In these interesting times, it is providing us with a long-overdue reason to change. What we need do is be receptive to it. Creative consciousness has already solved every issue before us. The only thing required of us is to let go of our false belief and misdirected faith and flow.

The power that has brought us this far will take us the rest of the way. Are we willing to stop competing so we can be open to the answer? As the Universe speaks, are we listening?

Notes

Notes

Aaaaah, Christmas
December 2008

When I was very young, my father bought me a train set for Christmas. It was marvelous.

In those days, we lived in a house heated by coal. In the basement, there was a coal chute and storage place. My dad and I took the new train downstairs and set it up next to the coal storage. What a great place it was–a warm, comfy area next to the furnace. Next to it, we set up two large sheets of plywood upon which we constructed my train set. We had rails running into the coal storage where we built a coal mine, then circled it back into a little town we created. There were balsa wood bridges, painted rivers and lakes, and scale buildings and scale people.

We would work for hours, putting everything in place, designing, building, and painting. There were little trees, little people, little trains, and little animals–and I loved it. It was my own little universe, a place where I could control everything.

I would mine the coal and deliver it to my own market. I ran the store, the feedlot, the farm, and the depot. I moved my people around from place to place and took good care of them. As time went on, I expanded the town, and it soon had lakes, fishing camps, a sawmill, and a used car lot. Immense bridges of balsa traversed torrential rivers, and there were train crossings with gates and a turn circle at the depot.

I still remember the passion and joy I felt. I would run home from school so I could play with my train. It was the focus of my life; it fulfilled me. It was a thing of awesome wonder. Then one day, unconsciously I am sure, I became aware I was real and that a world outside was calling me. The bigger life beckoned, and I left my cozy corner in the basement and went out to the real world where stores, feedlots, sawmills, and so much more existed.

I realize I have spent the last 50 years attempting to emulate the wonderful sense of purpose, passion, and joy I first discovered while playing with my Christmas present. I have attempted to find the same sense of completeness and connectedness in the world, to apply the same diligence, have the same vision, and enjoy the same creativity.

For me, Christmas is the story of awakening this sense in the individual. It is a story of becoming aware of the value, power, self-direction, creativity, and control of any person and the dedicated application and expression of it. I now think this is the true purpose of life–to awaken the light within ourselves so we may serve the world in a constructive, creative way. Happy holidays!

Notes

Notes

This Is the Time
January 2009

It may come as a surprise, but I write these articles well in advance of publication. One might think it is a challenge to write an article for January in August. Having done this, I am amazed at how quickly I can project forward five months. I am also amazed at the substance of said projection.

In Canada, January is a month of short days and cold weather. How peculiar that I can be sitting here in summer, projecting myself forward to such an inclement time of year. I can clearly imagine sitting in this exact spot with a dingy kind of light filtering in, dressed in long pants and a sweater with thermal underwear beneath, watching the snowfall. I will have just completed the Christmas season, given the mandatory "New Year" talk, eaten lots of turkey, and shoveled the driveway. I will have attended holiday parties and been back-slapped, kissed on the lips by strangers, and shaken hands 500 times. Hundreds of people will have half-heartedly wished me well and asked me about my resolutions and told me theirs.

Society will be in full marketing form claiming this month, somehow, has fantastic powers that will automatically catapult us all into a new vision of life. The hopes, aspirations, and good wishes for all will be a promise that this is the time to get that new start. January is the month it all begins. If only this could be true for August.

Well, maybe it is. Every moment is an opportunity to begin fresh. Maybe I could break with tradition and start a new plan, a new direction–today. If I could, I wonder where I would start. What does our teaching say? I am the creative agent in my experience. My every thought becomes a reality. What I experience is the fulfillment of my anticipation. My life is based on my attitude, and my perception reflects my expectations to a tee.

For me, January is a month of quiet retreat. It is a time to relax and digest the months preceding it. It is a time to sit by the fire and renew relationships, a time to read and contemplate, a time to celebrate the silence and relish the coming of spring. It is a time to enjoy and be grateful, reflecting on the wonder and miracle of life. It is a time to bask in friendships, cherish my connections, and renew my commitments.

I look forward to the beauty of the new-fallen snow, the brilliant light of the nights as the moon reflects on the whiteness of nature awaiting rebirth. It is a time of comfort food and warm clothes. It is a time to remember loved ones, to digest the intimacy and shared experiences of others. January is a time of renewal, a time of creativity, and a time of peace. Happy New Year.

Notes

Notes

The Spiritual Vote
February 2009

The majority of people on this planet are caring, compassionate, generous, and well meaning. Wherever you go, you will find most everyone supports the values and basic human rights we ourselves hold dear.

If you were to ask any population anywhere whether or not they support freedom, peace, education, a world where everyone has enough to eat, clean water, and safe conditions, you would find overwhelming agreement. If you were to ask any population if they wanted war or poverty, fear or horror, they would say no. If you asked whether they supported genocide, abuse, or terror, they would say no. So the question is, why are these things happening?

In the last few months we have seen an amazing change in the political atmosphere of the world. The collective unconscious works the same way. Articulated support in a common direction shifts the effect. In summary, the masses follow the most dominantly articulated purpose. Dr. Ernest Holmes put it this way: "Trained thought is more powerful than untrained thought."[1]

Just like in the political forum, consciousness requires that you show up to register your choice. If you do not go to the polls, your voice will not be heard. If you are reading this article, you are probably one of the ones who does show up, but we are still missing some six billion others.

Voting is a means to count the collective voice, and majority rules. Well-meaning and like-minded attitude does not count. We are a majority, but we have not found a way to get out the vote yet.

How do we get out the spiritual vote? We commit ourselves and encourage others to join and unite with organizations like ours that represent our opinions so we can accurately and effectively speak with a common voice.

There are at least two reasons we do not do this. First, as a movement, we are not united. Second, as individuals, we are not committed. There are thousands of organizations and groups who are quietly serving the cause of consciousness; unfortunately, they are often not connected to each other. As such, for a multitude of reasons, we are not cooperatively creating with each other.

In addition, as individuals, we do not understand the bigger stakes and bigger vision that is possible. There are more reasons not to participate in our own projected "stuff" than there are reasons to participate. They range from, "Sundays are my only day off," to, "I don't believe in church."

As a senior minister of a spiritual centre for the last 15 years, I have heard them all: "His message is great, but his voice is too squeaky"; "I certainly agree with the message but he uses the word God too often"; or, my all-time favourite, "I don't like someone in the congregation, so I won't go."

We need to let the world know that attendance is important. We also need to be clear that personal agendas and personal prejudices are effectively taking us out of the consciousnes electoral game.

Often, when I hear these excuses, I say: "So, you would rather sleep late than have world peace?" or, "You mean you're allowing your dislikes to perpetuate the misery of this world?" Harsh, yes, but true.

It is time for us to rise above our differences and tastes and go about our work of awakening humanity to its spiritual magnificence. The entire planet is counting on us.

Notes

1 - Holmes, E. (1938). *The Science of Mind. A philosophy, a faith, a way of life.* Penguin Putnam Inc: NY (p. 47)

Notes

Relatively Absolute
March 2009

In The Science of Mind, our founder, Dr. Ernest Holmes, states, "We wish to affirm relativity without destroying Absoluteness." He goes on to say, "This can be done only by realizing the relative is not a thing apart from, but is an experience in, the All-comprehending Mind."[1]

In light of this wisdom, I tell my students that my goal is not to become Absolute or to live solely in the relative. My intention, rather, is to blend the two in such a way that they mesh like gears coming together in harmony. If the Absolute, as Dr. Holmes claims, is Cause, and the relative is effect, it is my purpose to bring them together so they are one.

I consider the same to be true for all aspects of my life. I do not want to be masculine or feminine, I do not want to be right-brained or left, I do not want to be Eastern-minded or Western-minded, and I do not want to be ascetic or materialistic. I want to be balanced in every aspect of my life.

This intention extends into every part of my living: to be loving in the midst of animosity, present when preoccupied, alert while tired, generous while judicious, kind while irate, understanding while confused, compassionate while angry, and faithful while afraid. There are two keys that help me do this.

The first is awareness of my intention and rising above any temporary schism I might be experiencing in the moment. I do this by remembering that the relative is, as Dr. Holmes defines it, "That which depends upon something else",[2] while the Absolute is unlimited and unconditioned.

The second key is to be conscious that I have a choice. I must recognize how choice determines the direction in which I lean away from my desired balance. I always attempt to lean in the direction of the Absolute because there, I cannot make a mistake.

Finally, there is one other conscious practice I embody. I remind myself that this life–my life–is a gift; not something to be taken for granted. The gift of sharing the creative process of life with the Divine and to be a participant in playing consciously with the Infinite System of Creation is beyond words. The opportunity to play with God is such an awesome manifestation of everything good that I cannot help but play nice.

Notes

1 & 2 - Holmes, E. (1938). *The Science of Mind. A philosophy, a faith, a way of life.*
Penguin Putnam Inc: NY (p. 627)

Notes

Devotion
April 2009

Our philosophy has many facets, one of which is certainly self-discipline. By definition, self-discipline is the training of our mind and character.

Those who have succeeded in changing their minds from a core belief are more than aware of how challenging this can be. To accept a new paradigm of belief after 20, 30, 40 or more years of inculcation requires a tenacity and diligence that supersedes any average undertaking. However, discipline is only one facet of this teaching.

If we only rely on one tool to transform our consciousness, we are, in effect, creating the potential for unnecessary struggle. This is because there are other factors that contribute to who we are that are available to us, that can come into play if we invite them.

Luciano Pavarotti was quoted as saying, "People think I'm disciplined. It is not discipline. It is devotion. There is a great difference."[1] It is here that we find the most powerful tool we have in redefining and reconditioning our consciousness. Devotion is love given with one's whole heart and will. Its application to every aspect of our lives provides simplicity, ease, fulfillment, purpose, and meaning. It adds immeasurably to the value of life.

As a minister in the International Centers for Spiritual Living, the purpose and definition of my devotion is clear: "Awakening Humanity to Its Spiritual Magnificence." When I act from this devotion, I find struggle and challenge disappear. It answers for me every question imaginable around the what and why of my existence, and it acts as a beacon to light my way and apply my faith.

Devotion serves to clarify and prioritize everything I do. The only discipline left for me to undertake is to live, practice, and remember what is mine to do. Devotion simplifies my intentions and prioritizes my actions. It provides me with an anchor to live congruently with who I am. It draws everything I require to serve it and repels or brings into conscious thought everything unlike itself.

Devotion becomes the foundation of my relative life, and it awakens me to my own value and greatness. It is what I do when I teach, when I parent, when I lead, and when I follow. It grows, sustains, supports, and nourishes me. It is the Thing Itself, and it is who I am and who you are.

Notes

1 - Pavarotti, L. (n.d.) MyInspirational-Quotes.com. Retrieved June 23, 2010 from MyInspirational-Quotes.com website: http://www.myinspirational-quotes.com/end-procrastination/luciano-pavarotti.html

Notes

Stepping into Newness
May 2009

I watch my 15-month-old grandson toddle around my home learning something new every minute. If he misjudges a step, trips on a rug, or falls when he goes too fast, I make sure he is not hurt. I applaud him for moving forward and support him in his learning. I do not cajole, berate, or belittle him because he cannot run, talk, or jump. He is learning.

Dan Millman wrote:

> Every positive change–every jump to a higher level of energy and awareness–involves a rite of passage. Each time, to ascend to a higher rung on the ladder of personal evolution, we must go through a period of discomfort, of initiation. I have never found an exception.[1]

I have discovered I am usually more successful doing this with my grandson than I am with myself. I am not overly fond of change. Naturally, it is what I most need to do.

When change is indicated, I usually force myself to step into it because it is my rite of passage. The only thing stopping me is that period of discomfort.

I know my belief in the possibility of change without

discomfort, error, or falling off course is absurd. The very nature of "new" means doing something I have not done before. As such, the experiences and learning must be encountered to get from "a" to "b" or old to new.

To enter into a new paradigm, to adopt a new protocol, to create a new entity, to embody a new idea, to embark on a new course, or simply to endeavor to change is only challenging because of fear. Change is an opportunity to grow and become more effective. The only difference between a 15-month-old and me is that I have an expectation around who I am or who I believe others should perceive me to be.

My fear of making a mistake is hindered by this, so I am not always quick or comfortable in initiating change. I have even witnessed others who have refused to change because of those very fears.

What I know is that most of our expectations about ourselves are so bloated and enlarged that moving forward actually becomes a place of terror. When this occurs, we make the biggest mistake of all, i.e., endeavoring to stand still.

"new" means
doing something you have not done before . . .

The primary law of the Universe is expansion. When we do not face our fears, when we refuse to risk stepping into newness, we lose our pertinence in the scheme of life.

The disappointments we encounter by taking the risk are always based on the same thing. All disappointment is the result of a false expectation. Our unrealistic self-expectation cannot be used as a reason not to move forward.

We are here to learn. Through learning, we grow. Through growth, we create a new effect. Through effect, we learn, and the cycle begins again.

To break the cycle is to stop, and when we stop, we begin to atrophy. When we atrophy, we diminish, and when we diminish, we die. This is true in the life of the individual, the life of an organization, and the life of a society.

I will not let fear keep me from living. I refuse to stop growing no matter what anyone thinks of me. I am toddling as best as I can, and I know you are too.

Notes

_____

_____

_____

_____

_____

_____

_____

_____

_____

_____

1 - Millman, D. (1992). *No ordinary moments: A peaceful warrior's guide to daily life.* H.J. Kramer: Tiburon, CA.

Notes

Moving Forward in Faith
June 2009

Fear of failure is the single greatest deterrent to success. Far too often, those who capitulate to this fear remain frozen, static, and stuck. In so doing, they slow the evolution of humankind both consciously and developmentally. The first Law of the Universe is expansion. The adage, "Grow or die," proves correct in the physical, mental, emotional, and metaphysical reality of life. The most distressing part of this is that every forward step humankind or any individual has ever made in any field was preceded by a fall.

I once read an article about the physics of walking that described walking as controlled falling. As soon as I read this, I tested the claim, and I could see that every step forward was indeed preceded by an intentional surrender to falling.

Symbolically, the act of moving forward is really about letting go and falling, hopefully in a direction you have chosen. The act of covering any distance is about stringing a series of falls together for the purpose of arriving at a destination or goal. We let go, fall, replant, then stabilize and balance before repeating the process all over again.

As a people, we have reached a point where standing still is not working very well. It seems all of our systems, traditions, and ways of governing and running everything from our economy to foreign affairs is in need of review. We can remain immobile and watch while we disintegrate, or we can change direction and move forward. Perhaps the reason we are so slow to move is that we are afraid we will fail; ironically, we fail by not moving.

George Fowler wrote, "It is difficult to take 'fallen' seriously when where you've landed is with those who dance deep in the heart of a light-filled Universe."[1] It is time to be clear about what we are really afraid of. What we are witnessing in our individual lives, businesses, organizations, and nations is merely the manifestation of our greater good. Our reticence to totally renew what is not working stems from our fear that the next step will land us flat on our faces.

This is more an indicator of our distrust of the Universe than our fear of actually falling. It is time to have faith: faith in goodness, faith in beauty, faith in the calling, and faith in the Divine. It is time to adopt a different attitude, develop a new idea, and trust that That which has brought us this far will take us the rest of the way.

Notes

1 - Fowler, G. (1996). *Dance of a fallen monk: A journey to spiritual enlightenment.* Random House.

Notes

Prayer Work
July 2009

Spiritual Mind Treatment or affirmative prayer is the foundation of our teaching. No matter what form we teach or are taught, it is a recipe for inner communication with the All, which, of course, includes us.

Our churches and centres teach that we first acknowledge and embrace the Infinite. Then, we unify with It and direct It. We follow with an expression of gratitude that our good is already so. Finally, we release our word.

Our teaching also specifies that it is not the form of the prayer that creates our demonstration. Rather, it is our knowing and our faith.

I once heard a colleague compare teaching affirmative prayer to teaching someone to drive. He said he would not dream of getting in a car with an experienced driver and saying, "Now turn the key, put the car in gear, and give it some gas . . ." However, when teaching a new driver he would, of course, do all those things.

After driving for a while, it becomes autonomic and we do it as first nature. The same is true of affirmative prayer. After doing it for a while, it, too, becomes autonomic, which means we do it as first nature, and it requires little or no conscious initiation. Once the steps are embodied, practice takes it to its own inevitable conclusion.

I am now in the third semester of teaching the Science of Mind 100 series. One of the major objectives of this class is to teach people what Spiritual Mind Treatment is and to encourage them to use it constantly in their lives.

It is at this stage of the class, after they have had 20 or so weeks of the how and why of treatment, that I ask them to raise their hands if they believe treatment works. I am always gratified to see every hand enthusiastically thrown up high.

Then, I ask the students how many are treating daily, and it is interesting to see the reaction. Maybe half raise their hands, and half of those only raise them part of the way.

My next question is: "If you believe it works, why aren't you doing it?" The answers are as innumerable as the students responding, but the common denominator is always the same–it appears not to be as important as something else.

We have left behind the idea of a "Divine Director" who knows what is best. We have grown beyond our understanding of a "Cosmic Ruler" who dictates grace. We have dismissed any notion of a "Celestial Judge" that hands out rewards and punishment based on a subjective inclination established by current morality.

To paraphrase Dr. Ernest Holmes, spirit responds to the mind that knows it and directs it. Treatment is a tool to understand and change our old beliefs, and our beliefs become the form of our experience.

How is it that we can have hundreds of students understand that affirmative prayer works and still not use it? The answer, I fear, is written above. Far too many believe the practice and discipline of spiritual work is not as important as something else.

Here is my next question to my class: "What is more important than everything?" It only works if you work it.

Notes

_____

_____

_____

_____

_____

_____

_____

_____

_____

_____

_____

_____

_____

_____

_____

Notes

True Wealth
August 2009

With the so-called "economic situation" at the forefront these days, let us begin by clarifying our topic. The dictionary defines wealth as, "An abundance of worldly possessions."[1] To possess means, "to have as property or get control over."[1] Property is, "a thing or things owned, or the exclusive right to possess and use."[1]

As metaphysicians, we believe the essence of any form is not contained in the form itself but, rather, in the idea behind the form. As such, we may redefine wealth as, "the idea behind an abundance of things we own and have control over with an exclusive right to use." Being that the only value any form has is the essence and energy that lies behind it, it stands to reason there is only one thing anybody really owns, has control over, and has exclusive rights to–and that is our mind. There is only one asset any of us possess, and that is our Self.

Perhaps we get mixed up at times and assume the belief that we are a reflection of our wealth rather than seeing our wealth as a reflection of us. At times like this, it is easy to don an attitude of despondency and despair. Thank God, we know better.

Wealth is not that which controls us; it is that which we control. Wealth is a reflection of our beliefs, prejudices, opinions, imagination, and ideas. It is not our bank accounts, stock portfolios, pension plans, or material possessions. Wealth is the state of our minds, our attitudes, and our level of acceptance.

In the glossary of The Science of Mind, Dr. Ernest Holmes defines money as the "symbol of God's substance."[2] Since we believe God and Mind are synonymous, and since there is only one Mind and that Mind is our mind, it stands to reason money is the symbol of our substance. What is our substance? The dictionary, once again, defines it as, "The matter, stuff, and material of which a thing is made . . . the essential underlying reality of something." [1]

What has transpired over the past year in our economy, our markets, and our accounts has not subtracted even one cent from our substance. Our wealth is intact; it always has been and always will be. We do not require a bailout, and we do not require relief. The only thing we require is the clarity and vision to understand that our source is never dependent on the material in our lives, for it is a reflection of our beliefs.

I recall a situation my teacher, Dr. Tom Costa, shared with me once when he was faced with a monetary loss. He told me he suffered and fretted over it for several weeks until he realized that by doing so, he was depreciating his belief in abundance. When he realized this, he took action. He released his perceived loss to the Universe Itself, recognizing God as his only Source. Of course, the good came back to him pressed down and overflowing.

This is how I choose to handle my perceived situation. Right here and right now, I give my "mis-perceived" monetary loss joyfully, without strings, to the Universe Itself, knowing I am wealthy and prosperous, clear and complete, for I am my only asset and my substance is all substance. God is my only Source.

Notes

1 - *The Concise Oxford Dictionary of Current English* (1964). Edited by H.W. Fowler & F.G. Fowler based on the Oxford Dictionary, Fifth Edition Oxford, Clarendon Press.
2 - Holmes, E. (1938). *The Science of Mind. A philosophy, a faith, a way of life.* Penguin Putnam Inc: NY (p. 613)

Notes

Manifesting Love
September 2009

When I was a university student, I took a psychology course. In it, I discovered some disturbing statistics. Apparently, children who grow up in homes where physical violence is present are 80 percent more likely to behave violently toward their own children.

I grew up in a home where corporal punishment was practiced. As such, I decided when I had children, I would never use physical discipline–no matter what! My intention was, "The violence stops here."

In the decades since that decision and the birth of my two beautiful children, I have only broken that commitment once. To this day, I remember and regret it.

The incident occurred when my daughter, our firstborn, was around two years old. Our family was camping in California when my daughter and I were playing together, and in her exuberance, she ran away from me into a busy street.

My heart jumped, and I chased after her, which only made her run faster. Just as she entered the street I caught her, swung her around, and swatted her once on her diapered bottom, exclaiming something like, "Never run out in the street again! You hear me?"

Since that day, I have often tried to justify my simple act of abuse. I have said to myself, "It was for her own good." I have insisted, "It didn't really hurt her." I have even asked, "What else could I have done?" as though there was not another alternative.

Still, the truth remains. Giving her a spank on the bottom had little if nothing to do with her actions; it had everything to do with my motivation. There has never been a provocation to violence that was not motivated by the same reason–and that reason is fear.

Violent actions are predicated on fear. Knowing this, we could say domestic violence is all about fear, gang violence is all about fear, and wars are all about fear.

I once read that at the core of every human being, there are only two basic emotions: love and fear. Love is the absence of fear, and fear is the absence of love.

If I accept this as true and take it a step further, it seems natural that anything I fear can be neutralized with love. It stands to reason that which I fear requires love and becomes less fearful in direct proportion to how much love I give it.

If we choose to manifest a world where violence is as antiquated and unacceptable as some of the other erroneous beliefs our society has owned and relegated to the ridiculous, e.g., the Earth is flat, smoking is cool, then it is incumbent upon us to realize physical violence can never produce peaceful results. It is possible for us to change our minds and allow love to heal any appearance of fear. Love is the absence of fear . . .

Notes

Notes

I Do Know
October 2009

Dr. Raymond Charles Barker told the story of sitting quietly in his office one day when he heard a commotion. Suddenly, a woman he had never seen before pushed her way through his door, walked across the room, slapped a one-hundred-dollar bill on his desk, and demanded, "Get me a man!" Without another word, she strolled out. She knew what she wanted, and she got it.

Exactly one year later, the woman returned. Flinging another hundred dollars on the desk, she ordered, "Now, get rid of him!"

When you know what you want, you get it. If you do not like it, get something else.

The affirmations of the unconscious consist of many little phrases that numb our minds and justify our resistance to waking up. Many have formed a vocabulary that excuses us from living consciously and allows us to maintain self-imposed ignorance. These are affirmations we use daily, if not hourly. They are phrases that block our inquisitive natures and help sustain beliefs that do not serve us effectively. The most prevalent of these is, "I don't know."

Certainly, there are appropriate times to use this. Ask me the square root of 27,785.23 and I will truthfully respond,

"I don't know." There are many things for which I do not have a legitimate answer. However, there are many occasions on which that reply is used out of habit. Perhaps a more accurate answer would be, "I've never thought of it before," or "I don't care." At least then we have the opportunity to be honest with our questioners and ourselves.

As a practitioner, when meeting with clients, I usually sit and discuss their current life situations for a portion of time. They voice their issues and tell their stories while I sit and listen. At some point, I always ask, "What do you want?" Far too often, the answer is, "I don't know." That pretty much sums up why they have what they have and not what they want. This is true for me, too. It is true for all of us.

If I am not clear about what I want, and if I am not directing my energy toward what I desire because "I don't know" what it is, I should not be surprised if I demonstrate whatever is going around, so to speak. "I don't know" has become a convenient way to avoid being clear and an excuse not to be responsible.

If we do not know what we want, who does? The first step to awakening is to become clear about what we want so we may direct our energy toward manifesting it. I recall the old adage, "If I don't use my mind, someone else will." It is time to determine clearly what we want from life. I know what I want: for all of us to bring our magnificent potential into being.

Notes

Notes

Awakening the World
November 2009

In his 1943 paper entitled, "The Theory of Human Motivation,"[1] Abraham Maslow observed and listed a hierarchy of human needs. In essence, this list diarized his perception of the priorities of humanity and conscious evolution.

Maslow defined the first level of human need as physiological, i.e., the basic requirements necessary to sustain life such as food, water, and shelter. The second stage is safety, which deals with requirements for financial and personal safety as well as stability and access to resources for one's health and welfare.

The third level of his hierarchy is social, which includes friendship, intimacy, tribal connections, and religious groups.

The fourth is esteem, which takes into account acceptance, recognition, contribution, and self-value. The fifth is self-actualization, which is the motivation to realize one's own potential and possibility.

Most individuals who come to our Centers for Spiritual Living have pretty well taken care of steps one and two before they ever attend. As such, the third level is where we begin our educating process. We do this by developing safe, secure, and loving communities for our congregants so they may experience a sense of belonging and acceptance.

Everyone needs to know they are loved and wanted by others. From this foundation, we enter the fourth stage by providing a deep sense of self-esteem and self-respect, which draws from within individuals their own beauty, power, and skills. In this way, they come to recognize their innate value and contribution.

This tends to strengthen self-acceptance and self-value and propels individuals to the next step in conscious evolution, which is self-actualization. This is the motivation to realize one's own maximum potential and possibilities and is considered to be the only real motive, all other motives being its various forms. According to Maslow, this is the final need that manifests when all the lower-level needs have been satisfied.

With all the change we are witnessing in the world today, I believe we are on the edge of entering a societal model that, while still containing remnants of all the other stages, is nonetheless the existing step society is struggling to learn. New Thought is the most influential and organized system for disseminating the tools and knowledge necessary to educate the world in awakening the potential and possibilities of the human experience. However, this is not where our participation ends.

In Maslow's later years, he added a sixth stage to the hierarchy: self-transcendence.[2] This is the ability to be aware of the realm of being.

I suggest this is the state we refer to in our vision of, "Awakening Humanity to Its Spiritual Magnificence." It is about awakening individuals to a state of unity consciousness so they may experience what Maslow refers to as a "plateau experience" with all its corresponding expressions.

This is a state of illumination and insight. It is a state of cognition that realizes the potential of both the individual and world society. This cognition, Maslow predicted, will open the door to transformation of the individual and the world, even to the extent of changing the form.

This step is truly the awakening. This is what we must begin to model and project. It is time for us to step away from our preoccupation with the individual and step into the realization that our calling is to awaken the world as a whole.

As I speak, the International Centers for Spiritual Living and the United Centers for Spiritual Living are in a process of integration, of becoming one. International's vision is, "Awakening Humanity to Its Spiritual Magnificence;" United's is, "A World that Works for Everyone."

We can make this a world that works for everyone by awakening the world to its spiritual magnificence. We do this by facilitating the evolution of consciousness. Yes, it is up to us.

Notes

1 - Maslow, A.H. (1943). A theory of human motivation. *Psychological Review*, 50, 370-396.

2 - Maslow, A.H. (1969). The farther reaches of human nature. *Journal of Transpersonal Psychology*, 1(1), 56-66.

Notes

The Leading Edge
of New Thought
December 2009

I want to state that we are a bottom-up organization and that we operate from the body. We are purely a 100-percent democratic organization.

It is important for me to stress this over and over again because we act as one mind, one body, and one life within the One. We come forward with a consciousness of agreement to expand and grow our teachings.

Last year, I stated the object of the president's office was to reach out and take us to a place of leadership within New Thought. I am happy to say that in the past year, what has happened, actually, is the development of stronger and more sustainable relationships with the United Centers for Spiritual Living (UCSL), Associated New Thought Network (ANTN), Universal Life, Unity, Associated Global New Thought (AGNT), and International New Thought Alliance (INTA).

We have made a connection that binds us to each and every one of them, and we share with them as we step forward as the leading edge of New Thought. As such, as the leading edge, it is incumbent upon us to continue to move forward in this spirit, maintaining the principles we hold true. The tenets upon which we operate are inclusiveness and communication–always in principle. We will maintain and continue this in the coming year.

This past year, we said we were going to be the leaders in New Thought. We said we were going to step forward and take our rightful place within that greater movement in order to be able to guide and direct the truth and awaken humanity to its spiritual magnificence, which is our vision. Stepping into 2010, it is our responsibility to model this awakening.

Notes

Notes

This is Who We Are
January 2010

What is happening in form in the world around us is this: humanity is waiting for us to step forward. When we talk about 60 million "cultural creatives" waiting to join our teaching, we are selling ourselves short. There are over six billion people who are waiting to learn, understand, and move into that which we teach and the principles we espouse by any name whatsoever.

I saw a bumper sticker this morning that read, "God is too big to fit into one religion." It could not have been more accurate.

God is too big to fit into one religion; therefore, we must fit into God. We have to understand that in terms of the world around us, it is not the effect we need to deal with. Instead, we could decide to make ourselves bigger than the effect rather than falling down to the size of it.

The world is ripe for change. It is ripe, and it is waiting for us to step forward and move into it.

We have been called to do something major. This time, we cannot back down from it.

We need a greater idea in our lives. So much is going on in our movement. So much is going on in our organization.

Every worldly idea needs to be taken to the world. Every worldly idea is an opportunity for us to serve.

We know this in principle. We know this in life. We know this in light, and we know it within the very body of who we are as a teaching and as individuals.

It is time to step into our power. We can choose to rise above what the form of the world outside looks like. We can freely and openly move forward.

There is nothing wrong with the world out there. I know with absolute certainty that it is up to us, as metaphysicians, to raise our consciousness above effect and move into the world in the power with which we are gifted. This is who we are.

Notes

About the Author
Dr. Kenneth D. Gordon

Dr. Kenn and his wife, Dr. Deborah Gordon, are the founding spiritual directors of the Centre for Spiritual Living in Kelowna, B.C. The Gordons began their Science of Mind studies in 1986, taking classes and ministerial training in Palm Desert, California. Once they graduated, their dream was to bring the Science of Mind teaching to their hometown and the Okanagan region, and in 1993 they did just that. Their vision statement is "Awakening Humanity to Its Spiritual Magnificence."

As gifted and inspiring speakers, devoted teachers and spiritual counsellors, the Gordons' commitment to serving others extends far beyond the geographical boundaries of their Centre.

Dr. Kenn is currently the President of International Centers for Spiritual Living™. In 2005, he was named Minister of the Year and received his Doctor of Religious Science.

Dr. Kenn's lectures are currently available on audio CD. They will be available in print soon. For more information, contact us at www.cslkelowna.com.